GUIDELINES FOR THE ASSESSMENT
OF GENERAL DAMAGES
IN PERSONAL INJURY CASES

GUIDELINES FOR THE ASSESSMENT OF GENERAL DAMAGES IN PERSONAL INJURY CASES

Fourth Edition

Compiled for the
Judicial Studies Board

by

**John Cherry, QC; Edwin Glasgow CBE, QC;
D. A. K. Hughes, Solicitor; R. J. Sutcliffe, Solicitor;
His Honour Judge Roger Cox**

Foreword by The Right Hon. Lord Justice Henry
Chairman, Judicial Studies Board

BLACKSTONE
PRESS LIMITED

First published in Great Britain 1992 by Blackstone Press Limited, Aldine Place, London W12 8AA. Telephone 0181-740 2277

First edition 1992
Reprinted 1992
Reprinted 1993
Reprinted 1994
Second edition 1994
Reprinted 1994
Reprinted 1996
Third edition 1996
Reprinted 1997
Fourth edition 1998

ISBN: 1 85431 756 3

British Library Cataloguing in Publication Data
A CIP catalogue record for this book is available from the British Library.

Typeset by Style Photosetting Limited, Mayfield, East Sussex
Printed by Ashford Colour Press, Gosport, Hampshire

Contents

vi

Foreword by Lord Justice Henry

This is now the fourth edition of this book. The first three came warmed by the praise of three successive Masters of the Rolls. Lord Donaldson saw the first edition's utility as an aid to the assessment of general damages for pain, suffering and loss of the amenities of life as a distillation of 'the conventional wisdom contained in the reported cases' supplemented by 'the collective experience of the Working Party set up by the Judicial Studies Board who compiled it'. Sir Thomas Bingham found in it 'the broad effect of the current consensus in relation to different classes of injury' indicating 'the range of awards likely to be made, on the basis of past awards and current practice, in the ordinary run of case'. Lord Woolf saw it as facilitating settlements as well as achieving greater consistency and certainty in the decisions of judges.

As that chronological sequence shows, the work has succeeded in what it set out to do: to present a snap-shot of the general level of such damages reflected by judicial decisions and settlements influenced by them. What the Working Party wish to make clear is that their guidelines are emphatically not intended to promote any views as to what the level of damages ought to be either now or in the future: these are guidelines simply recording what is happening today. There is currently a lively debate initiated by the Law Commission as to what the level of such damages ought to be. But that debate is not addressed here: this work reflects the market as it presently is in the court and corridors of our legal system.

The Judicial Studies Board is as proud of this initiative as it is grateful to Judge Cox and his distinguished team for the enormous amount of work in reducing a multitude of cases into such a user-friendly format. To simplify without distortion requires good judgment and a lot of work. Their success with this book has greatly improved the quality and consistency of justice in these cases. Judges and advocates alike have cause to be grateful.

Lord Justice Henry
Chairman, Judicial Studies Board
23 October 1998

Foreword to the First Edition
by Lord Donaldson of Lymington

Paradoxical as it may seem, one of the commonest tasks of a judge sitting in a civil court is also one of the most difficult. This is the assessment of general damages for pain, suffering or loss of the amenities of life. Since no monetary award can compensate in any real sense, these damages cannot be assessed by a process of calculation. Yet whilst no two cases are ever precisely the same, justice requires that there be consistency between awards.

The solution to this dilemma has lain in using the amount of damages awarded in reported cases as guidelines or markers and seeking to slot the particular case into the framework thus provided. This is easier stated than done, because reports of the framework cases are scattered over a variety of publications and not all the awards appear, from the sometimes brief reports, to be consistent with one another. Furthermore some of the older cases are positively misleading unless account is taken of changes in the value of money and the process of revaluation is far from being an exact science.

It was against this background that the Judicial Studies Board set up a working party under the chairmanship of Judge Roger Cox to prepare 'Guidelines for Assessment of General Damages in Personal Injury Cases'. It was not intended to represent, and does not represent, a new or different approach to the problem. Nor is it intended to be a 'ready reckoner' or in any way to fetter the individual judgment which must be brought to bear upon the unique features of each particular case. What it is intended to do, and what it does quite admirably, is to distil the conventional wisdom contained in the reported cases, to supplement it from the collective experience of the working party and to present the result in a convenient, logical and coherent form.

There can be no doubt about the practical value of this report and it has been agreed by the four Heads of Division that it shall be circulated to all judges, recorders and district judges who may be concerned with the assessment of general damages in personal injury cases. We also consider that it should be made available to the two branches of the practising profession and to any others who would be assisted by it.

Judges and practitioners will, as always, remain free to take full account of the amount of damages awarded in earlier cases, but it is hoped that with the publication of this report this will less often be necessary. They will also need to take account of cases reported after the effective date of the working party's report since that report, while to some extent providing a new baseline is not intended to, and could not, freeze the scale of damages either absolutely or in relative terms as between different categories of loss.

May I convey my sincere congratulations to the authors upon the excellent way in which they have performed their task.

Lord Donaldson of Lymington
25 March 1992

Introduction

In producing the fourth edition of this book the Working Party set up by the Judicial Studies Board in 1990 has looked anew at definitions and brackets, though it must be said that in many areas there are no decisions to indicate that the original figures need revision save to the extent that inflation must be considered.

The members of the Working Party are sincerely grateful for the comments, contributions and criticisms which have been received from friends and colleagues at all levels of the profession. They feel the need, however, perhaps more than before, to remind themselves and those who use and comment on these guidelines (for that is all that they are intended to be) of the task that they were originally given by the Civil and Family Committee of the Judicial Studies Board. That was and remains to distil guidelines from awards which have in fact been made; it is not and never was to promote any views which they may have about what the level of those awards *ought* to be. Thus, in working through the material which has been collated (and it is substantial) and in considering the generous help which has been offered by others, the Working Party has had frequently to resist the temptation to adjust or alter particular figures or brackets simply because its members, and sometimes others who have greater experience, think that they *seem* to be 'out of line'.

The Working Party has therefore concentrated on actual awards made by the courts or the Criminal Injuries Compensation Board. It has of course looked carefully, as it did for previous editions, at settlements the details of which its members have been made aware of, especially where they have been the subject of court approval. In view of the help which has been received from so many quarters it is necessary to say something about the care with which such settlements have been regarded, whether the information has come from the collective experience of the Working Party or from the contributions of others.

In recent years the process of settling actions for damages for personal injuries in all but the most straightforward of cases has been complicated by doubts about the basis on which multipliers for future losses were to be calculated. While these doubts have now been resolved by the decision of the House of Lords in *Wells* v *Wells* [1998] 3 WLR 329 they resulted in settlements being agreed for general damages for pain suffering and loss of amenity which did not necessarily reflect a ruthlessly objective evaluation of those elements in the assessment of the overall value of the case. General damages for pain and suffering, particularly in the most serious cases, often represent but a comparatively small part of the global award or settlement. Thus, it is the experience of the Working Party, and of those from whom soundings have been taken, that parties have been prepared to agree settlements including figures for pain and suffering where the overall compromise figure has been attractive, despite the fact that one or other of the parties did not consider that a court would have been likely to award as general damages on a contested trial of the action the sum which was agreed in respect of that element. Accordingly, the members of the Working Party have been careful not to allow themselves to be over-influenced by information received about settlement figures which do not appear to accord with the results of their researches into decided cases. This apparent reluctance to move away from the brackets which reflect actual decisions should not be taken as indicating any ingratitude on the part of the Working Party for the information which has been provided, for all of it has been carefully considered. It would be most unfortunate if these guidelines were to make it more difficult to agree on an overall figure which experienced practitioners honestly and reasonably felt to be right in a particular case. Rather, it is hoped that these guidelines will be used, as the Master of the Rolls indicated in his Foreword to the third edition, as 'the starting off point rather than the last word . . . in any particular case'.

The Working Party has not overlooked the danger that guidelines may come to be regarded as self-fulfilling prophesies. It should be emphasised that it is for the courts to set the levels of damages and for this book to reflect them. It is not possible in a work such as this minutely to define every injury or state of affairs which will be compensated and it would defeat the purpose of this book were its definitions to be stretched by others to apply to that for which they do not provide. If it is the case that the brackets which have been distilled from the cases are no longer thought to be appropriate, it must be for the courts and not for this Working Party to signal a change.

The members of the Working Party would like to express their gratitude to all those who have contributed to their researches, to the Judicial Studies Board for its unstinting support and, in particular, to Andrea Dowsett, its publications co-ordinator, for the immense help which she has given.

The figures in this edition are based on awards up until August 1998.

1. Injuries involving Paralysis

(a) Quadriplegia   £120,000 to £150,000

The level of the award within the bracket will
be affected by the following considerations:

(i)   the extent of any residual movement;

(ii)   the presence and extent of pain;

(iii) depression;

(iv)   age and life expectancy.

The top of the bracket will be appropriate only
where there is significant effect on senses.

(b) Paraplegia   £90,000 to £110,000

The level of the award within the bracket will
be affected by the following considerations:

(i)   the presence and extent of pain;

(ii)   depression;

(iii) age and life expectancy.

The presence of increasing paralysis or the
degree of risk that this will occur, for example
from syringomyelia, might take the case
above this bracket.

2. Head Injuries

(A) Brain Damage

(a) Very Severe Brain Damage £110,000 to £150,000

In the most severe cases the injured person will have a degree of insight. There may be some ability to follow basic commands, recovery of eye opening and return of sleep and waking patterns and postural reflex movement. There will be little, if any, evidence of meaningful response to environment, little or no language function, double incontinence and the need for full-time nursing care.

The level of the award within the bracket will be affected by:

(i)   the degree of insight;

(ii)   life expectancy;

(iii)   the extent of physical limitations.

The top of the bracket will be appropriate only where there is significant effect on the senses.

Where there is a persistent vegetative state and/or death occurs very soon after the injuries were suffered and there has been no awareness by the injured person of his or her

4

condition the award will be solely for loss of amenity and will fall substantially below the above bracket.

(b) Moderately Severe Brain Injury   £90,000 to £110,000

The injured person will be very seriously disabled. There will be substantial dependence on others and a need for constant care. Disabilities may be physical, for example, limb paralysis, or cognitive, with marked impairment of intellect and personality. Cases otherwise within (a) above may fall into this bracket if life expectancy has been greatly reduced.

The level of the award within the bracket will be affected by the following considerations:

(i)   the degree of insight;

(ii)   life expectancy;

(iii) the extent of physical limitations;

(iv)   the degree of dependence on others;

(v)   behavioural abnormality.

(c) Moderate Brain Damage

This category is distinguished from (b) by the fact that the degree of dependence is markedly lower.

(i)   Cases in which there is moderate to severe intellectual deficit, a personality change, an effect on sight, speech and senses with a significant risk of epilepsy.   £65,000 to £90,000

(ii) Cases in which there is a moderate to modest intellectual deficit, the ability to

work is greatly reduced if not removed
and there is some risk of epilepsy.   £40,000 to £65,000

   (iii) Cases in which concentration and memory are affected, the ability to work is
reduced, where there is a small risk of
epilepsy and any dependence on others
is very limited.   £20,000 to £40,000

(d) Minor Brain Damage   £7,500 to £20,000

In these cases the injured person will have
made a good recovery and will be able to take
part in normal social life and to return to work.
There may not have been a restoration of all
normal functions so there may still be persisting problems such as poor concentration and
memory or disinhibition of mood, which may
interfere with lifestyle, leisure activities and
future work prospects.

The level of the award within the bracket will
be affected by:

  (i)   the extent and severity of the initial
injury;

  (ii) the extent of any continuing, and possible permanent, disability;

  (iii) the extent of any personality change.

(B) Minor Head Injury   £1,000 to £6,000

In these cases brain damage, if any, will have
been minimal.

The level of the award will be affected by the
following considerations:

  (i)   the severity of the initial injury;

  (ii) the period taken to recover from any
severe symptoms;

(iii)   the extent of continuing symptoms;

(iv)   the presence or absence of headaches.

(C) Epilepsy

(a) Established Grand Mal   £45,000 to £65,000

The level of the award within the bracket will
be affected by the following factors:

(i)   whether attacks are successfully con-
trolled by medication and the extent to
which the need for medication is likely
to persist;

(ii)   the extent to which the appreciation of
life is blunted by such medication;

(iii)   the effect on working and/or social life;

(iv)   the existence of associated behavioural
problems.

(b) Established Petit Mal   £25,000 to £55,000

The level of the award within the bracket will
be affected by the following factors:

(i)   whether attacks are successfully con-
trolled by medication and the extent to
which the need for medication is likely
to persist;

(ii)   the extent to which the appreciation of
life is blunted by such medication;

(iii)   the effect on working and/or social life;

(iv)   the existence of associated behavioural
problems.

(c) Other Epileptic Incidents   £5,000 to £12,500

Cases where there are one or two discrete epileptic episodes but there is no risk of recurrence beyond that applicable to the population at large. The level of the award within the bracket will be affected by the extent of any consequences of the attacks on, for example, education, sporting activities, working and social life, and their duration.

3. Psychiatric Damage

In part (A) of this chapter some of the brackets contain an element of compensation for post-traumatic stress disorder. This is of course not a universal feature of cases of psychiatric injury and hence a number of the awards upon which the brackets are based did not reflect it. Where it does figure any award will tend towards the upper end of the bracket. Cases where post-traumatic stress disorder is the sole psychiatric condition are dealt with in part (B) of this chapter.

(A) Psychiatric Damage Generally

The factors to be taken into account in valuing claims of this nature are as follows:

(i) the injured person's ability to cope with life and work;

(ii) the effect on the injured person's relationships with family, friends and those with whom he or she comes into contact;

(iii) the extent to which treatment would be successful;

(iv) future vulnerability;

(v) prognosis;

(vi) whether medical help has been sought.

(a) Severe £25,000 to £50,000

In these cases the injured person will have marked problems with respect to factors (i) to (iv) above and the prognosis will be very poor.

(b) Moderately Severe £9,000 to £25,000

In these cases there will be significant problems associated with factors (i) to (iv) above but the prognosis will be much more optimistic than in (a) above. While there are awards which support both extremes of this bracket, the majority were between £15,000 and £17,500.

(c) Moderate £3,000 to £9,000.

While there may have been the sort of problems associated with factors (i) to (iv) above there will have been marked improvement by trial and the prognosis will be good.

(d) Minor £500 to £2,250

The level of the award will take into consideration the length of the period of disability and the extent to which daily activities and sleep were affected.

(B) Post-traumatic Stress Disorder

Cases within this category are exclusively those where there is a specific diagnosis of a reactive psychiatric disorder in which characteristic symptoms are displayed following a psychologically distressing event which was outside the range of normal human experience and which would be markedly distressing to almost anyone. The guidelines below have been compiled by reference to cases which variously reflect the criteria established in the 4th edition of *Diagnostic and Statistical Manual of Mental Disorders* (DSM IV). The symptoms affect basic functions such as breathing, pulse rate and bowel and/or bladder control. They also involve persistent re-experience of the relevant event, difficulty in controlling temper, in concentrating and sleeping, and exaggerated startled [sic: startle] response.

(a) Severe £28,500 to £40,000

Such cases will involve permanent effects which prevent the injured person from working at all or at least from functioning at anything approaching the pre-trauma level. All aspects of the life of the injured person will be badly affected.

(b) Moderately Severe £12,500 to £25,000

This category is distinct from (a) above because of the better prognosis which will be for some recovery with professional help. However, the effects are still likely to cause significant disability for the foreseeable future.

(c) Moderate £3,500 to £9,500

In these cases the injured person will have largely recovered and any continuing effects will not be grossly disabling.

(d) Minor £1,750 to £3,500

In these cases a virtually full recovery will have been made within one to two years and only minor symptoms will persist over any longer period.

4. Injuries affecting the Senses

(A) Injuries affecting Sight

(a) Total Blindness and Deafness £150,000

Such cases must be considered as ranking with the most devastating injuries.

(b) Total Blindness £105,000

(c) Loss of Sight in One Eye with Reduced Vision in the Remaining Eye

    (i) Where there is serious risk of further deterioration in the remaining eye, going beyond the normal risk of sympathetic ophthalmia. £42,500 to £75,000

    (ii) Where there is reduced vision in the remaining eye and/or additional problems such as double vision. £28,500 to £48,500

(d) Total Loss of One Eye £26,000 to £30,000

The level of the award within the bracket will depend on age and cosmetic effect.

(e) Complete Loss of Sight in One Eye £22,500 to £25,000

This award takes account of the risk of sympathetic ophthalmia. The upper end of the bracket is appropriate where there is scarring in the region of the eye which is not sufficiently serious to merit a separate award.

(f) Cases of serious but incomplete loss of vision in one eye without significant risk of loss or reduction of vision in the remaining eye, or where there is constant double vision.   £11,500 to £18,250

(g) Minor but permanent impairment of vision in one eye, including cases where there is some double vision, which may not be constant.   £6,000 to £10,000

(h) Minor Eye Injuries   £1,850 to £4,000

In this bracket fall cases of minor injuries, such as being struck in the eye, exposure to fumes including smoke, or being splashed by liquids, causing initial pain and some interference with vision, but no lasting effects.

(i) Transient Eye Injuries   £1,000 to £1,850

In these cases the injured person will have recovered completely within a few weeks.

(B) Deafness

The word 'deafness' is used to embrace total and partial hearing loss. In assessing awards for hearing loss regard must be had to the following:

    (i)   whether the injury is one that has an immediate effect, allowing no opportunity to adapt, or whether it occurred over a period of time, as in noise exposure cases;

    (ii)   whether the injury or disability is one which the injured person suffered at an early age so that it has had or will have an effect on his or her speech, or is one that is suffered in later life;

13

(iii)   whether the injury or disability affects balance;

(iv)   in cases of noise-induced hearing loss (NIHL) age is of particular relevance as noted in paragraph (d) below.

(a)   Total Deafness and Loss of Speech   £47,500 to £60,000

Such cases arise, for example, where deafness has occurred at an early age (for example, rubella infection) so as to prevent or seriously to affect the development of normal speech.

(b)   Total Deafness   £40,000 to £47,500

The lower end of the bracket is appropriate for cases where there is no speech deficit or tinnitus. The higher end is appropriate for cases involving both of these.

(c)   Total Loss of Hearing in One Ear   £15,000 to £21,500

Cases will tend towards the higher end of the bracket where there are associated problems, such as tinnitus, dizziness or headaches.

(d)   Partial Hearing Loss/Tinnitus

This category covers the bulk of deafness cases which usually result from exposure to noise over a prolonged period. The disability is not to be judged simply by the degree of hearing loss; there is often a degree of tinnitus present. Age is particularly relevant because impairment of hearing affects most people in the fullness of time and impacts both upon causation and upon valuation.

(i)   Severe tinnitus/hearing loss.   £13,750 to £21,250

(ii)   Moderate tinnitus/hearing loss.   £7,000 to £13,750

14

(iii)	Mild tinnitus with some hearing loss.	£6,000 to £7,000
(iv)	Slight or occasional tinnitus with slight hearing loss.	£3,500 to £6,000

Tariff schemes agreed between unions and insurers have been operating for some years. These tariffs provide scales for compensation measured by precise decibel loss and degree of tinnitus at differing ages. In assessing the above brackets, which reflect decided cases, these schemes have not been adopted because none of them has achieved general judicial approval and they are currently being replaced by simpler schemes based on conventional brackets of compensation for decibel loss, principally affected by age.

(C) Impairment of Taste and Smell

(a)	**Total Loss of Taste and Smell**	£18,250
(b)	**Total Loss of Smell and Significant Loss of Taste**	£15,500 to £18,000

It must be remembered that in nearly all cases of loss of smell there is some impairment of taste. Such cases fall into the next bracket.

(c)	**Loss of Smell**	£12,000 to £15,500
(d)	**Loss of Taste**	£9,000 to £12,000

5. Injuries to Internal Organs

(A) Chest Injuries

This is a specially difficult area because the majority of awards relate to industrial *disease* as distinct from traumatic *injury* and the level of the appropriate award for lung disease necessarily, and often principally, reflects the prognosis for what is frequently a worsening condition and/or the risk of the development of secondary sequelae (such as mesothelioma in asbestos-related cases). Cases of traumatic damage to, or loss of, a lung are comparatively rare: the range is as wide as £1,000 to £65,000.

The levels of awards within the brackets set out below will be affected by:

(i) age and gender;

(ii) scarring;

(iii) the effect on the capacity to work and enjoy life;

(iv) the effect on life expectancy.

(a) The very worst case will be of total removal of one lung and/or serious heart damage with serious and prolonged pain and suffering and permanent significant scarring. £45,000 to £65,000

16

(b) Traumatic injury to chest, lung(s) and/or heart causing permanent damage, impairment of function, physical disability and reduction of life expectancy. £30,000 to £45,000

(c) Damage to chest and lung(s) causing some continuing disability. £15,000 to £25,000

(d) A relatively simple injury (such as a single penetrating wound) causing some permanent damage to tissue but with no significant long-term effect on lung function. £6,000 to £8,500

(e) Toxic fume/smoke inhalation, leaving some residual damage, not serious enough permanently to interfere with lung function. £2,750 to £6,000

(f) Injuries leading to collapsed lungs from which a full and uncomplicated recovery is made. £1,000 to £2,500

(g) Fractures of ribs, causing serious pain and disability over a period of weeks only. Up to £1,750

(B) Lung Disease

Most of the reported cases are of asbestos-related disease but, save for asthma (which is dealt with separately), the brackets set out below are intended to encompass all lung disease cases irrespective of causation. In many cases falling under this head provisional awards will be appropriate save at the upper end of the range where serious disabling consequences will already be present and the prognosis is likely to be relatively clear.

(a) For a young person with serious disability where there is a probability of progressive worsening leading to premature death. £45,000 to £55,000

(b) Mesothelioma (typically in an older person), lung cancer or asbestosis causing severe impairment both of function and of quality of life. £35,000 to £45,000

(c) Disease causing significant and worsening lung function and impairment of breathing, prolonged and frequent coughing, sleep disturbance and restriction of physical activity and employment — including the more serious cases of pleural thickening.   £25,000 to £35,000

(d) Breathing difficulties (short of disabling breathlessness) requiring fairly frequent use of an inhaler; where there is inability to tolerate smoky environment; significant pleural thickening and an uncertain prognosis but already significant effect on social and working life.   £15,000 to £25,000

(e) Bronchitis and wheezing; pleural plaques or thickening not causing serious symptoms; little or no serious or permanent effect on working or social life; varying levels of anxiety about the future.   £10,000 to £15,000

(f) Some slight breathlessness with no effect on working life and the likelihood of substantial and permanent recovery within a few years of the exposure to the cause or the aggravation of an existing condition.   £5,000 to £10,000

(g) Provisional awards for cases otherwise falling within (f), or the least serious cases within (e) where the provisional award excludes any risk of malignancy or of asbestosis.   £2,500 to £5,000

(h) Temporary aggravation of bronchitis or other chest problems resolving within a very few months.   £1,000 to £2,500

(C) Asthma

(a) Severe and permanent disabling asthma, causing prolonged and regular coughing, disturbance of sleep, severe impairment of physical

18

activity and enjoyment of life and where employment prospects, if any, are grossly restricted. £20,000 to £30,000

(b) Chronic asthma causing breathing difficulties, the need to use an inhaler from time to time and restriction of employment prospects, with uncertain prognosis. £12,500 to £20,000

(c) Bronchitic wheezing, affecting working or social life, with the likelihood of substantial recovery within a few years of the exposure to the cause. £9,000 to £12,500

(d) Restrictive airways dysfunction syndrome (RADS). Relatively mild asthma-like symptoms resulting from a single exposure to harmful irritating vapour. £5,000 to £9,000

(e) Mild asthma, bronchitis, colds and chest problems (usually resulting from unfit housing or similar exposure, particularly in cases of young children) treated by a general practitioner and resolving within a few months. Up to £2,250

(D) Digestive System

The risk of associated damage to the reproductive organs is frequently encountered in cases of this nature and requires separate consideration.

(a) Severe damage with continuing pain and discomfort. £20,000 to £28,500

(b) Serious non-penetrating injury causing long-standing or permanent complications, for example, severe indigestion, aggravated by physical strain. £8,000 to £13,250

(c) Penetrating stab wounds or industrial laceration or serious seat-belt pressure cases. £3,000 to £6,000

19

(E) Reproductive System: Male

(a) Impotence

(i) Total impotence and loss of sexual function and sterility in the case of a young man.

The level of the award will depend on:

(1) age;

(2) psychological reaction and the effect on social and domestic life.   In the region of £62,500

(ii) Impotence which is likely to be permanent, in the case of a middle-aged man with children.   £20,000 to £35,000

(b) Cases of sterility usually fall into one of two categories: surgical, chemical and disease cases (which involve no traumatic injury or scarring) and traumatic injuries (frequently caused by assaults) which are often aggravated by scarring.

(i) The most serious cases merit awards approaching   £58,500

(ii) The bottom of the range is the case of the much older man and merits an award of about   £9,000

(c) An uncomplicated case of infertility without any aggravating features for a young man without children.   £26,500 to £32,500

(d) A similar case but involving a family man who might have intended to have more children.   £11,500 to £14,500

(e) Cases where the infertility amounts to little more than an 'insult'.   In the region of £3,000

20

(F) Reproductive System: Female

The level of awards in this area will typically depend on:

  (i) whether or not the affected woman already has children and/or whether the intended family was complete;

  (ii) scarring;

  (iii) depression or psychological scarring;

  (iv) whether a foetus was aborted.

(a) Infertility whether by reason of injury or disease, with severe depression and anxiety, pain and scarring.   £50,000 to £70,000

(b) Infertility without any medical complication and where the injured person already has children. The upper end of the bracket is appropriate in cases where there is significant psychological damage.   £8,500 to £17,250

(c) Infertility where the injured person would not have had children in any event (for example, because of age).   £3,000 to £6,000

(d) Failed sterilisation leading to unwanted pregnancy where there is no serious psychological impact or depression.   £3,000 to £4,000

(G) Kidney

(a) Serious and permanent damage to or loss of both kidneys.   £70,000 to £85,000

(b) Where there is a significant risk of future urinary tract infection or other total loss of natural kidney function the range is up to   £28,500

21

Such cases will invariably carry with them substantial future medical expenses, which in this field are particularly high.

(c) Loss of one kidney with no damage to the other.　　　　　　　　　　　　　　　£14,500 to £20,000

(H) Bowels

(a) Total loss of natural function and dependence on colostomy, depending on age.　　　　Up to £65,000

(b) Severe abdominal injury causing impairment of function and often necessitating temporary colostomy (leaving disfiguring scars) and/or restriction on employment and on diet.　　£21,000 to £32,000

(c) Penetrating injuries causing some permanent damage but with an eventual return to natural function and control.　　　　　　　　　£6,000 to £11,500

(I) Bladder

It is perhaps surprising that awards in cases of loss of bladder function have often been higher than awards for injury to the bowels. This is probably because bladder injuries frequently result from carcinogenic exposure (typically to antioxidants such as Nonox S in the rubber industry). The reported decisions are seriously out of date and merely increasing them to relect inflation may be misleading.

(a) Complete loss of function and control.　　Up to £60,000

(b) Serious impairment of control with some pain and incontinence.　　　　　　　　　£28,500 to £35,000

(c) Where there has been almost a complete recovery but some fairly long-term interference with natural function.　　　　　　£11,500 to £14,500

The cancer risk cases still occupy a special category and can properly attract awards at the top of the ranges even where natural function continues for the time being. However, these cases will now more appropriately be dealt with by provisional awards of a low level (£5,000) unless the foreseeable outcome is clear. Once the prognosis is firm and reliable the award will reflect any loss of life expectancy, the level of continuing pain and suffering and most significantly the extent to which the injured person has to live with the knowledge of the consequences which his or her death will have for others. The appropriate award for the middle-aged family man or woman whose life expectancy is reduced by 15 or 20 years is £25,000 to £35,000.

(J) Spleen

(a) Loss of spleen where there is continuing risk of internal infection and disorders due to the damage to the immune system. £10,000 to £12,500

(b) Where the above risks are not present or are minimal. £2,000 to £4,000

(K) Hernia

(a) Continuing pain and/or limitation on physical activities, sport or employment. £7,000 to £11,500

(b) Direct (where there was no pre-existing weakness) inguinal hernia, with some risk of recurrence. £3,250 to £4,250

(c) Uncomplicated indirect inguinal hernia with no other associated abdominal injury or damage. £1,500 to £3,000

6. Orthopaedic Injuries

(A) Neck Injuries

There is a very wide range of neck injuries. At the highest end of the spectrum is the injury which shatters a life and leaves the injured person very severely disabled. This may have a value of up to £65,000. At the other end of the spectrum is the minor strain which causes the injured person to be off work for a very short period and to suffer symptoms for only a few weeks. This type of injury would attract an award of between £1,000 and £1,500. The neck injury giving rise to symptoms for no more than a couple of weeks would attract no more than about £500.

(a) Severe

(i) Neck injury associated with incomplete paraplegia or resulting in permanent spastic quadriparesis or where the injured person, despite wearing a collar 24 hours a day for a period of years, still has little or no movement in the neck and suffers severe headaches which have proved intractable. £65,000

(ii) Injuries which give rise to disabilities which fall short of those in (a)(i) above but which are of considerable severity; for example, permanent damage to the brachial plexus. £30,000 to £55,000

(iii) Injuries causing severe damage to soft tissues and/or ruptured tendons. They result in significant disability of a permanent nature. The precise award depends on the length of time during which the most serious symptoms are ameliorated, and on the prognosis.   In the region of £25,000

(iv) Injuries such as fractures or dislocations which cause severe immediate symptoms and which may necessitate spinal fusion. They leave markedly impaired function or vulnerability to further trauma, and some limitation of activities.   £12,000 to £15,500

(b) Moderate

(i) Cases involving whiplash or wrenching-type injury and disc lesion of the more severe type resulting in cervical spondylosis, serious limitation of movement, permanent or recurring pain, stiffness or discomfort and the possible need for further surgery or increased vulnerability to further trauma.   £6,500 to £12,000

(ii) Injuries which may have exacerbated or accelerated some pre-existing unrelated condition. There will have been a complete recovery from the effects of the injury within a few years. This bracket will also apply to moderate whiplash injuries where the period of recovery has been fairly protracted and where there remains an increased vulnerability to further trauma.   £3,500 to £6,500

(c) Minor

Minor soft tissue and whiplash injuries and the like where symptoms are moderate and a full recovery takes place within at most two years.   Up to £3,500

(B) Back Injuries

Relatively few back injuries which do not give rise
to paralysis command awards above about £22,500.
In those that do there are special features.

(a) Severe

(i) Cases of the most severe injury which
do not involve paralysis but where there
may be very serious consequences not
normally found in cases of back injury,
such as impotence or double incontinence.

£45,000 to £70,000

(ii) Cases which have special features tak-
ing them outside any lower bracket
applicable to orthopaedic injury to the
back. Such features include impaired
bladder and bowel function, severe
sexual difficulties and unsightly scarring and the possibility of future
surgery.

In the region of £37,500

(iii) Cases of disc lesions or fractures of
discs or of vertebral bodies where,
despite treatment, there remain disabilities such as continuing severe pain and
discomfort, impaired agility, impaired
sexual function, depression, personality
change, alcoholism, unemployability
and the risk of arthritis.

£18,500 to £30,000

(b) Moderate

(i) Cases where any residual disability is of
less severity than that in (a)(iii) above.
The bracket contains a wide variety of
injuries. Examples are a case of a crush
fracture of the lumbar vertebrae where

there is a substantial risk of osteoarthritis and constant pain and discomfort with impairment of sexual function; that of a traumatic spondylolisthesis with continuous pain and a probability that spinal fusion will be necessary; or that of a prolapsed intervertebral disc with substantial acceleration of back degeneration. £13,250 to £18,500

(ii) Many frequently encountered injuries to the back such as disturbance of ligaments and muscles giving rise to backache, soft tissue injuries resulting in exacerbation of an existing back condition or prolapsed discs necessitating laminectomy or resulting in repeated relapses. The precise figure depends upon the severity of the original injury and/or whether there is some permanent or chronic disability. £6,000 to £13,250

(c) **Minor**

Strains, sprains, disc prolapses and soft tissue injuries from which a full recovery has been made or which result only in minor continuing disability or as a result of which there has been acceleration or exacerbation of pre-existing unrelated conditions for a fairly brief period of time. Up to £6,500

(C) Injuries to the Pelvis and Hips

The most serious of injuries to the pelvis and hip can be as devastating as a leg amputation and accordingly will attract a similar award of damages. Such cases apart, the upper limit for these injuries will generally be in the region of £32,500. Cases where there are specific sequelae of exceptional severity would call for a higher award.

(a) Severe

(i) Extensive fractures of the pelvis involving, for example, dislocation of a low
back joint and a ruptured bladder, or a
hip injury resulting in spondylolisthesis
of a low back joint with intolerable pain
and necessitating spinal fusion. Inevi-
tably there will be substantial residual
disabilities such as a complicated
arthrodesis with resulting lack of bladder and bowel control, sexual dysfunction or hip deformity making the use of
a calliper essential.   £35,000 to £55,000

(ii) Injuries only a little less severe than in
(a)(i) above but with particular distin-
guishing features lifting them above
any lower bracket. Examples are: (a)
fracture dislocation of the pelvis involving both ischial and pubic rami and
resulting in impotence; or (b) traumatic
myositis ossificans with formation of
ectopic bone around the hip.   £28,500 to £35,000

(iii) Many injuries fall within this bracket: a
fracture of the acetabulum leading to
degenerative changes and leg instability requiring an osteotomy and the
likelihood of hip replacement surgery in
the future; the fracture of an arthritic
femur or hip necessitating hip replacement; or a fracture resulting in a hip
replacement which is only partially
successful so that there is a clear risk of
the need for revision surgery.   £18,500 to £24,000

(b) Moderate   £12,750 to £18,500

Significant injury to the pelvis or hip but any
permanent disability is not major and any
future risk not great.

| **(c)** | **Injuries of Limited Severity** | £6,000 to £12,750 |

These cases usually involve hip replacement. Where it has been carried out wholly success-fully the award will tend to the top of the bracket, but the bracket also includes cases where hip replacement is anticipated in the foreseeable future.

| **(d)** | **Minor Injuries** | Up to £6,000 |

These are cases where despite injury there is no residual disability.

(D) Shoulder Injuries

Unless they are associated with severe neck, back or arm injury, shoulder injuries tend to attract modest awards of well under £10,000.

| **(a)** | **Serious** | £6,000 to £9,000 |

Dislocation of the shoulder and damage to the lower part of the brachial plexus causing pain in shoulder and neck, aching in elbow, sensory symptoms in the forearm and hand, and weakness of grip.

| **(b)** | **Moderate** | £3,750 to £6,000 |

Frozen shoulder with limitation of movement and discomfort with symptoms persisting for between one and two years.

| **(c)** | **Minor** | £2,000 to £3,750 |

Soft tissue injury to shoulder with consider-able pain but almost complete recovery in less than a year.

| **(d)** | **Fracture of Clavicle** | £1,500 to £3,250 |

The level of the award will depend on whether union is anatomically displaced.

(E) Amputation of Arms

(a) Loss of both arms   £95,000 to £115,000

There is no recent case to offer guidance but the effect of such an injury is to reduce a person with full awareness to a state of considerable helplessness.

(b) Loss of One Arm

(i) Arm Amputated at the Shoulder   Not less than £60,000

(ii) Above-elbow Amputation   £48,000 to £55,000

A shorter stump may create difficulties in the use of a prosthesis. This will make the level of the award towards the top end of the bracket. Amputation through the elbow will normally produce an award at the bottom end of the bracket.

(iii) Below-elbow Amputation   £42,500 to £48,000

Amputation through the forearm with residual severe organic and phantom pains would attract an award at the top end of the bracket.

The value of such an injury depends upon:

(i) whether the amputation is above or below the elbow. The loss of the additional joint adds greatly to the disability;

(ii) whether or not the amputation was of the dominant arm;

(iii) the intensity of any phantom pains.

(F) Other Arm Injuries

(a) Severe Injuries   £42,500 to £55,000

Injuries which fall short of amputation but
which are extremely serious and leave the
injured person little better off than if the arm
had been lost; for example, a serious brachial
plexus injury.

(b) Injuries resulting in Permanent and
Substantial Disablement   £18,500 to £27,500

Serious fractures of one or both forearms
where there is significant permanent residual
disability whether functional or cosmetic.

(c) Less Severe Injury   £9,000 to £18,500

While there will have been significant disabilities, a substantial degree of recovery will
have taken place or will be expected.

(d) Simple Fractures of the Forearm   £3,000 to £9,000

Uncomplicated fractures of the radius and/or
ulna with a complete recovery within a short
time would justify an award of £3,000.
Injuries resulting in modest residual disability
or deformity would merit an award towards
the upper end of this bracket.

(G) Injuries to the Elbow

(a) A Severely Disabling Injury   £18,250 to £25,000

(b) Less Severe Injuries   £7,500 to £15,000

Injuries causing impairment of function but
not involving major surgery or significant
disability.

(c) Moderate or Minor Injury   Up to £6,000

Most elbow injuries fall into this category. They comprise simple fractures, tennis elbow syndrome and lacerations; i.e. those injuries which cause no permanent damage and do not result in any permanent impairment of function.

(H) Wrist Injuries

(a) Injuries resulting in complete loss of function in the wrist, for example, where an arthrodesis has been performed.   £22,500 to £27,500

(b) Injury resulting in significant permanent disability, but where some useful movement remains.   £11,750 to £18,500

(c) Less severe injuries where these still result in some permanent disability as, for example, a degree of persisting pain and stiffness.   £6,000 to £11,750

(d) Where recovery is complete the award will rarely exceed   £5,000

(e) An uncomplicated Colles' fracture.   £3,500

(I) Hand Injuries

The hands are cosmetically and functionally the most important component parts of the upper limbs. The loss of a hand is valued not far short of the amount which would be awarded for the loss of the arm itself. The upper end of any bracket will generally be appropriate where the injury is to the dominant hand.

(a) Total or Effective Loss of Both Hands £60,000 to £80,000

Serious injury resulting in extensive damage to both hands such as to render them little more than useless will justify an award of £60,000. The top of the bracket is applicable where no effective prosthesis can be used.

(b) Serious Damage to Both Hands £25,000 to £37,500

Such injuries will have given rise to permanent cosmetic disability and significant loss of function.

(c) Total or Effective Loss of One Hand £42,500 to £48,750

This bracket will apply to a hand which was crushed and thereafter surgically amputated or where all fingers and most of the palm have been traumatically amputated. The upper end of the bracket is indicated where the hand so damaged was the dominant one.

(d) Amputation of Index and Middle and/or Ring Fingers £28,500 to £40,000

The hand will have been rendered of very little use and such grip as remains will be exceedingly weak.

(e) Serious Hand Injuries Up to £28,500

Such injuries will, for example, have reduced the hand to about 50 per cent capacity. Included would be cases where several fingers have been amputated but rejoined to the hand leaving it clawed, clumsy and unsightly, or amputation of some fingers together with part of the palm resulting in gross diminution of grip and dexterity and gross cosmetic disfigurement.

(f) Severe Fractures to Fingers   Up to £17,500

These may lead to partial amputations and result in deformity, impairment of grip, reduced mechanical function and disturbed sensation.

(g) Total Loss of Index Finger   £9,000

This is the maximum figure for this injury.

(h) Partial Loss of Index Finger   £5,850 to £8,500

This bracket also covers cases of injury to the index finger giving rise to disfigurement and impairment of grip or dexterity.

(i) Fracture of Index Finger   £4,250 to £5,850

This level is appropriate where a fracture has mended quickly but grip has remained impaired, there is pain on heavy use and osteoarthritis is likely in due course.

(j) Total Loss of Middle Finger   £7,500

(k) Serious Injury to Ring or Middle Fingers   £7,000 to £7,750

The top of this bracket is the maximum figure for serious injury involving either of these fingers. Fractures or serious injury to tendons causing stiffness, deformity and permanent loss of grip or dexterity will fall within this bracket.

(l) Loss of the Terminal Phalanx of the Ring or Middle Fingers.   £2,000 to £3,500

(m) Amputation of Little Finger.   £4,000 to £5,850

(n) Loss of Part of the Little Finger

This is appropriate where the remaining tip is
sensitive.   £2,000 to £2,750

(o) **Amputation of Ring and Little Fingers.** £10,500

(p) **Amputation of the Terminal Phalanges of the Index and Middle Fingers.**

This is appropriate where there is some further injury e.g., to the fourth finger. Such injury will involve scarring, restriction of movement and impairment of grip and fine handling. £11,750

(q) **Fracture of One Finger** £1,000 to £1,750

There will have been a complete recovery within a few weeks.

(r) **Loss of Thumb** £17,000 to £26,000

(s) **Very Serious Injury to Thumb** £9,500 to £17,000

This bracket is appropriate where the thumb has been severed at the base and grafted back leaving a virtually useless and deformed digit, or where the thumb has been amputated through the metacarpophalangeal joint.

(t) **Serious Injury to the Thumb** £6,000 to £8,000

Such injuries may involve amputation of the tip, nerve damage or fracture necessitating the insertion of wires as a result of which the thumb is cold and ultra-sensitive and there is impaired grip and loss of manual dexterity.

(u) **Moderate Injuries to the Thumb** £4,500 to £6,000

These are injuries such as those necessitating arthrodesis of the interphalangeal joint or causing damage to tendons or nerves. Such injuries result in impairment of sensation and function and cosmetic deformity.

(v) Severe Dislocation of the Thumb   £2,000 to £3,000

(w) Minor Injuries to the Thumb   In the region of £2,000

Such an injury would be a fracture which has recovered in six months except for residual stiffness and some discomfort.

(x) Trivial Thumb Injuries   £1,000

These may have caused severe pain for a very short time but will have resolved within a few months.

(y) Vibration White Finger

This is a particular form of Raynaud's phenomenon caused by prolonged exposure to vibration. Degrees of severity are measured both on the Taylor–Pelmear Scale and on the Stockholm Scale (for the neurological aspects). From the Taylor–Pelmear Scale the relevant categories are:

(i) extensive blanching of most fingers with episodes in summer and winter of such severity as to necessitate changing occupation to avoid exposure to vibration;

(ii) extensive blanching with episodes in summer and winter resulting in interference at work, at home and with hobbies and social activities;

(iii) blanching of one or more fingers with numbness, usually occurring only in winter and causing slight interference with home and social activities;

(iv) blanching of one or more fingertips with or without tingling or numbness.

The top of the bracket (£15,000 or more) would normally represent the most disabled stage 3/4 case on the Taylor–Pelmear Scale ((i) to (ii) above). The position within the bracket depends upon:

(i)   length and severity of attacks and symptoms;

(ii)   extent and/or severity and/or rapidity of deterioration;

(iii)   age and prognosis.

In some cases these factors are more important than the stage the disease has reached.

The brackets can best be defined and valued as follows:

(i)	**Most Serious**	£10,000 to £16,000
(ii)	**Serious**	£7,500 to £10,000
(iii)	**Moderate**	£2,500 to £7,500
(iv)	**Minor**	Up to £2,500

(J) Work-related Upper Limb Disorders

This section covers a range of upper limb injury in the form of the following pathological conditions:

(a) Tenosynovitis: inflammation of synovial sheaths of tendons usually resolving with rest over a short period. Sometimes this condition leads to continuing symptoms of loss of grip and dexterity.

(b) De Quervain's tenosynovitis: a form of tenosynovitis, rarely bilateral, involving inflammation of the tendons of the thumb.

(c) Stenosing tenosynovitis: otherwise, trigger finger/thumb: thickening tendons.

(d) Carpal tunnel syndrome: constriction of the median nerve of the wrist or thickening of surrounding tissue. It is often relieved by a decompression operation.

(e) Epicondylitis: inflammation in the elbow joint: medial = golfer's elbow; lateral = tennis elbow.

The brackets below apply to all these conditions but the level of the award is affected by the following considerations regardless of the precise condition:

(i)   are the effects bilateral or one sided?

(ii)   the level of symptoms, i.e., pain, swelling, tenderness, crepitus;

(iii)   the ability to work;

(iv)   the capacity to avoid the recurrence of symptoms;

(v)   surgery.

(a) Continuing bilateral disability with surgery and loss of employment. £105,00 to £11,000

(b) Continuing, but fluctuating and unilateral symptoms. £7,000 to £7,500

(c) Symptoms resolving in the course of two years £4,000 to £4,500

(d) Complete recovery within a short period £1,000 to £1,500

(K) Leg Injuries

(a) Amputations

(i) Total Loss of Both Legs £95,000 to £110,000

This is the appropriate award where both legs are lost above the knee and

38

particularly if near to the hip leaving one or both stumps less than adequate to accommodate a useful prosthesis.

(ii) **Below-knee Amputation of Both Legs** £80,000 to £105,000

The top of the bracket is appropriate where both legs are amputated just below the knee. Amputations lower down result in a lower award.

(iii) **Above-knee Amputation of One Leg** £42,500 to £60,000

The area within the bracket within which the award should fall will depend upon such factors as the level of the amputation; the severity of phantom pains; whether or not there have been any problems with a prosthesis and any side effects such as depression or back-ache.

(iv) **Below-knee Amputation of One Leg** £40,000 to £55,000

The straightforward case of a below-knee amputation with no complications would justify an award at the bottom of this bracket. At or towards the top of the range would come the traumatic amputation which occurs in a devastating accident, where the injured person remained fully conscious, or cases where attempts to save the leg led to numerous unsuccessful operations so that amputation occurred years after the event.

(b) **Severe Leg Injuries**

(i) **The Most Serious Injuries short of Amputation** £42,500 to £57,500

Some injuries, although not involving amputation, are so severe that the courts have awarded damages at a comparable level. Such injuries would include extensive degloving of the leg, where there is gross shortening of the leg or where fractures have not united and extensive bone grafting has been undertaken.

(ii) Very Serious £25,000 to £37,500

Injuries leading to permanent problems with mobility, the need for crutches for the remainder of the injured person's life; injuries where multiple fractures have taken years to heal and have led to serious deformity and limitation of movement, or where arthritis has developed in a joint so that further surgical treatment is likely.

(iii) Serious £18,250 to £25,000

Serious injuries to joints or ligaments resulting in instability, prolonged treatment, a lengthy period of non-weight-bearing, the near certainty that arthritis will ensue; injuries involving the hip, requiring arthrodesis or hip replacement, extensive scarring. To justify an award within this bracket a combination of such features will generally be necessary.

(iv) Moderate £13,250 to £18,250

This bracket includes severe, complicated or multiple fractures. The level of an award within the bracket will be influenced by the period off work; the presence or risk of degenerative changes; imperfect union of fractures, muscle wasting; limited joint movements; instability in the knee; unsightly scarring or permanently increased vulnerability to future damage.

(c) Less Serious Leg Injuries

(i) **Fractures from which an Incomplete Recovery is Made** £8,500 to £13,250

The injured person will be left with a metal implant and/or defective gait, a limp, impaired mobility, sensory loss, discomfort or an exacerbation of a pre-existing disability.

(ii) **Simple Fracture of a Femur with no Damage to Articular Surfaces** Up to £7,000

(iii) **Simple Fractures and Soft Tissue Injuries** Up to £4,250

At the top of the bracket will come simple fractures of the tibia or fibula from which a complete recovery has been made. Below this level fall a wide variety of soft-tissue injuries, lacerations, cuts, bruising or contusions, all of which have recovered completely or almost so and any residual disability is cosmetic or of a minor nature.

(L) Knee Injuries

Knee injuries fall within a bracket extending from a few hundred pounds for a simple twisting injury up to £40,000 or more where there have been considerable problems leading to an arthrodesis.

(a) Severe

(i) Serious knee injury where there has been disruption of the joint, gross ligamentous damage, lengthy treatment, considerable pain and loss of function and an arthrodesis has taken place or is inevitable.

£32,000 to £42,500.

(ii) Leg fracture extending into the knee joint causing pain which is constant, permanent, limiting movement or impairing agility and rendering the injured person prone to osteoarthritis and the risk of arthrodesis.

£24,000 to £32,000

(iii) Less severe injuries than those in (a)(ii) above and/or injuries which result in less severe disability. There may be continuing symptoms by way of pain and discomfort and limitation of movement or instability or deformity with the risk that degenerative changes may occur in the long term as a result of damage to the kneecap, ligamentous or meniscal injury or muscular wasting.

£12,750 to £20,000

(b) Moderate

(i) Injuries involving dislocation, torn cartilage or meniscus or which accelerate symptoms from a pre-existing condition but which additionally result in minor instability, wasting, weakness or other mild future disability.

£7,000 to £12,750

(ii) This bracket includes injuries similar to those in (b)(i) above, but less serious, and also lacerations, twisting or bruising injuries. Where recovery has been complete the award is unlikely to exceed £3,000. Where there is continuous aching or discomfort, or occasional pain the award will be towards the upper end of the bracket.

Up to £6,500

(M) Ankle Injuries

The vast majority of ankle injuries are worth significantly less than £10,000. The ceiling, however, is about £32,000. This will be appropriate where the degree of disablement is very severe.

(a) Very Severe £23,500 to £32,000

Examples of injuries falling within this bracket are limited and unusual. They include cases of a transmalleolar fracture of the ankle with extensive soft-tissue damage resulting in deformity and the risk that any future injury to the leg might necessitate a below-knee amputation, or cases of bilateral ankle fractures causing degeneration of the joints at a young age so that arthrodesis is necessary.

(b) Severe £15,000 to £23,500

Injuries necessitating an extensive period of treatment and/or a lengthy period in plaster or where pins and plates have been inserted and there is significant residual disability in the form of ankle instability, severely limited ability to walk. The level of the award within the bracket will be determined in part by such features as a failed arthrodesis, regular sleep disturbance, unsightly scarring and any need to wear special footwear.

(c) Moderate £6,500 to £12,750

Fractures, ligamentous tears and the like which give rise to less serious disabilities such as difficulty in walking on uneven ground, awkwardness on stairs, irritation from metal plates and residual scarring.

(d) Modest Injuries   Up to £6,500

The less serious, minor or undisplaced fractures, sprains and ligamentous injuries. The
level of the award within the bracket will be
determined by whether or not a complete
recovery has been made and, if recovery is
incomplete, whether there is any tendency for
the ankle to give way, and whether there is
scarring, aching or discomfort or the possibility of later osteoarthritis.

(N) Achilles Tendon

(a) Most Serious   £17,250 to £19,000

Severance of the tendon and the peroneus
longus muscle giving rise to cramp, swelling
and restricted ankle movement necessitating
the cessation of active sports.

(b) Serious   £11,750 to £14,500

Where complete division of the tendon has
been successfully repaired but there is residual
weakness, a limitation of ankle movements, a
limp and residual scarring and where further
improvement is unlikely.

(c) Moderate   £7,000 to £8,500

Complete division of the tendon but where its
repair has left no significant functional disability.

(d) Minor   £3,500 to £4,750

A turning of the ankle resulting in some
damage to the tendon and a feeling of being
unsure of ankle support.

(O) Foot Injuries

(a) Amputation of Both Feet
£70,000 to £80,000

This injury is treated similarly to below-knee amputation of both legs because the common feature is loss of a useful ankle joint.

(b) Amputation of One Foot
£37,000 to £48,750

This injury is also treated as similar to a below-knee amputation because of the loss of the ankle joint.

(c) Very Severe
£37,000 to £48,750

To fall within this bracket the injury must produce permanent and severe pain or really serious permanent disability. Examples would include the traumatic amputation of the fore-foot where there was a significant risk of the need for a full amputation and serious exacerbation of an existing back problem, or cases of the loss of a substantial portion of the heel so that mobility was grossly restricted.

(d) Severe
£21,500 to £31,000

Fractures of *both* heels or feet with a substantial restriction on mobility or considerable or permanent pain. The bracket will also include unusually severe injury to a single foot resulting, for example, in heel fusion, osteoporosis, ulceration or other disability preventing the wearing of ordinary shoes. It will also apply in the case of a drop foot deformity corrected by a brace.

(e) Serious
£12,000 to £18,500

Towards the top end of the bracket fall cases such as those of grievous burns to both feet requiring multiple operations and leaving disfiguring scars and persistent irritation. At the lower end of the bracket would be those injuries less severe than in (d) above but leading to fusion of foot joints, continuing pain from traumatic arthritis, prolonged treatment and the future risk of osteoarthritis.

(f)	**Moderate**	£6,500 to £12,000

Displaced metatarsal fractures resulting in permanent deformity and continuing symptoms.

(g)	**Modest**	Up to £6,500

Simple metatarsal fractures, ruptured ligaments, puncture wounds and the like. Where there are continuing symptoms, such as a permanent limp, pain or aching, awards between £3,250 and £6,500 would be appropriate. Straightforward foot injuries such as fractures, lacerations, contusions etc. from which complete or near complete recovery is made would justify awards of £3,250 or less.

(P) Toe Injuries

(a)	**Amputation of All Toes**	£17,250 to £25,750

The position within the bracket will be determined by, for example, whether or not the amputation was traumatic or surgical and the extent of the loss of the forefoot together with the residual effects on mobility.

(b)	**Amputation of the Great Toe**	In the region of £14,500

(c)	**Severe Toe Injuries**	£6,500 to £9,000

This is the appropriate bracket for severe crush injuries, falling short of the need for amputation or necessitating only partial amputation. It also includes bursting wounds and injuries resulting in severe damage and in any event producing significant continuing symptoms.

(d)	**Serious Toe Injuries**	£4,500 to £6,500

Such injuries will be serious injuries to the great toe or crush and multiple fractures of two or more toes. There will be some permanent disability by way of discomfort, pain or sensitive scarring to justify an award within this bracket. Where there have been a number of unsuccessful operations or persisting stabbing pains, impaired gait or the like the award will tend towards the top end of the bracket.

(e)	**Moderate Toe Injuries**	Up to £4,500

These injuries include relatively straightforward fractures or the exacerbation of a pre-existing degenerative condition. Only £3,000 or less would be awarded for straightforward fractures of one or more toes with complete resolution within a short period of time and less still for minor injuries involving lacerations, cuts, contusions and bruises, in respect of all of which there would have been a complete or near complete recovery.

7. Facial Injuries

The assessment of general damages for facial injuries is an extremely difficult task, there being two elements which complicate the award.

First, while in most of the cases dealt with below the injuries described are skeletal, many of them will involve an element of disfigurement or at least cosmetic disability.

Secondly, in cases where there is a cosmetic element the courts have invariably drawn a distinction between the awards of damages to males and females, the latter attracting the higher awards.

The subject of burns is not dealt with separately, because burns of any degree of severity tend to be so devastating as to be invariably at the upper ends of the brackets.

In the guidance which follows some effort has been made to distinguish these types of cases but the above considerations must always be borne in mind. Where there is a cosmetic element care must be taken to endeavour to remain broadly within the guidelines which are extracted from reported decisions where the tribunal has had the advantage of seeing and hearing the injured person and has been able to make a subjective assessment.

(A) Skeletal Injuries

(a)   **Le Fort Fractures of Frontal Facial Bones**   £11,500 to £17,500

(b)   **Multiple Fractures of Facial Bones**   £7,250 to £11,500

Involving some facial deformity of a permanent nature.

(c)   **Fracture of Nose**

(i)   Serious fractures requiring a number of operations and resulting in permanent damage to airways and/or facial deformity.   £5,000 to £8,500

(ii)   Displaced fracture where recovery complete but only after surgery.   £1,850 to £2,250

(iii)   Displaced fracture requiring no more than manipulation.   £1,250 to £1,500

(iv)   Simple undisplaced fracture with full recovery.   £750 to £1,000

(d)   **Fractures of Cheekbones**

(i)   Serious fractures requiring surgery but with lasting consequences such as paraesthesia in the cheeks or the lips or some element of disfigurement.   £4,750 to £7,500

(ii)   Simple fracture of cheekbones for which some reconstructive surgery is necessary but from which there is a complete recovery with no or only minimal cosmetic effects.   £2,000 to £3,000

(iii)   Simple fracture of cheekbone for which no surgery is required and where a complete recovery is effected.   £1,150 to £1,450

(e) Fractures of Jaws

(i) Very serious multiple fractures followed by prolonged treatment and permanent consequences, including severe pain, restriction in eating, paraesthesia and/or the risk of arthritis in the joints. £14,250 to £21,250

(ii) Serious fracture with permanent consequences such as difficulty in opening the mouth or with eating or where there is paraesthesia in the area of the jaw. £8,500 to £14,250

(iii) Simple fracture requiring immobilisation but from which recovery is complete. £3,000 to £4,000

(f) Damage to Teeth

In these cases there will generally have been a course of treatment. The amounts awarded will vary according to the extent and/or the degree of discomfort of such treatment. It will often be necessary to award a lump sum in respect of the cost of future dental treatment.

(i) Loss of or serious damage to several front teeth. £4,000 to £5,000

(ii) Loss of two front teeth. £2,000 to £2,750

(iii) Loss of one front tooth. £1,000 to £1,750

(iv) Loss of or damage to back teeth: per tooth: £500 to £850

(B) Facial Disfigurement

In this class of case the distinction between male and female and the subjective approach are of particular significance.

(a) **Females**

    (i)   **Very Severe Facial Scarring**

        In a relatively young woman (teens to
        early 30s) where the cosmetic effect is
        very disfiguring and the psychological
        reaction severe.   £22,500 to £42,500

    (ii)   **Less Severe Scarring**

        Where the disfigurement is still sub-
        stantial and where there is a significant
        psychological reaction.   £14,500 to £22,500

    (iii) **Significant Scarring**

        Where the worst effects have been or
        will be reduced by plastic surgery leav-
        ing some cosmetic disability and where
        the psychological reaction is not great
        or, having been considerable at the
        outset, has diminished to relatively
        minor proportions.   £8,500 to £14,500

    (iv) **Less Significant Scarring**

        In these cases there may be but one scar
        which can be camouflaged or, though
        there is a number of very small scars the
        overall effect is to mar but not markedly
        to affect the appearance and the reaction
        is no more than that of an ordinarily
        sensitive young woman.   £2,000 to £6,500

(b) **Males**

    (i)   **Very Severe Facial Scarring**

        These are to be found especially in
        males under thirty, where there is per-
        manent disfigurement even after plastic
        surgery and a considerable element of
        psychological reaction.   £14,500 to £30,000

(ii) Severe Facial Scarring

This will have left moderate to severe
permanent disfigurement.   £8,500 to £14,500

(iii) Significant but not Severe Scarring

Such scars will remain visible at con-
versational distances.   £4,250 to £8,500

(iv) Relatively Minor Scarring

Such scarring is not particularly prom-
inent except on close inspection.   £2,000 to £4,250

(v) Trivial Scarring

In these cases the effect is minor only.   £850 to £1,600

8. Scarring to Other Parts of the Body

This is an area in which it is not possible to offer much useful guidance. The principles are the same as those applied to cases of facial disfigurement and the brackets are broadly the same. It must be remembered that many of the physical injuries already described involve some element of disfigurement and that element is of course taken into account in suggesting the appropriate bracket. There remain some cases where the element of disfigurement is the predominant one in the assessment of damages. Where the scarring is not to the face or is not usually visible then the awards will tend to be lower than those for facial or readily visible disfigurement.

The effects of burns will normally be regarded as more serious since they tend to cause a greater degree of pain and to lead to greater disfigurement.

There is, however, one area in which an almost 'conventional' figure has emerged. In cases where an exploratory laparotomy has been performed but no significant internal injury has been found the award for the operation and the inevitable scar is of the order of £4,000. The situation rarely occurs and when it falls to be valued it is usually by the Criminal Injuries Compensation Board.

9. Damage to Hair

(a) Damage to hair in consequence of defective permanent waving, tinting or the like, where the effects are tingling or 'burning' of the scalp causing dry, brittle hair, which breaks off and/or falls out, leading to distress, depression, embarrassment and loss of confidence, and inhibiting social life. In the more serious cases thinning continues and the prospects of regrowth are poor or there has been total loss of areas of hair and regrowth is slow.   £3,250 to £5,250

(b) Less serious versions of the above where symptoms are fewer or only of a minor character; also, cases where hair has been pulled out leaving bald patches. The level of the award will depend on the length of time taken before regrowth occurs.   £1,850 to £3,250

Index

Printed in the United Kingdom
by Lightning Source UK Ltd.
125176UK00001BA/1-9/A